POP CULTURE BIOS

# ARIANA
# GRANDE

FROM ACTRESS TO CHART-TOPPING SINGER

HEATHER E. SCHWARTZ

Lerner Publications Company
MINNEAPOLIS

To my loving in-laws, Connie
and Phil Schwartz

Lerner Publications Company
A division of Lerner Publishing Group, Inc.
241 First Avenue North
Minneapolis, MN 55401 USA

For reading levels and more information, look up this title at
www.lernerbooks.com.


Library of Congress Cataloging-in-Publication Data

Schwartz, Heather E.
     Ariana Grande : from actress to chart-topping singer / by
Heather E. Schwartz.
        pages    cm. — (Pop culture bios)
     Includes index.
     ISBN 978-1-4677-3669-5 (lib. bdg. : alk. paper)
     ISBN 978-1-4677-4730-1 (eBook)
     1. Grande, Ariana—Juvenile literature.  2. Singers—United
States—Biography—Juvenile literature.  3. Actresses—United
States—Biography—Juvenile literature.  I. Title.
ML3930.G724S38  2015
782.42164092—dc23 [B]                          2013051367


Manufactured in the United States of America
1 – PC – 7/15/14

# INTRODUCTION

Ariana (RIGHT) stands with the cast
of Nickelodeon's Victorious.

By the time Ariana Grande attended the 2013 American Music Awards, she was no stranger to the spotlight. Still, she was shaking in her Sergio Rossi shoes. For one thing, she was set to perform for an audience that included music's biggest stars: Lady Gaga, One Direction, Justin Timberlake, Rihanna, and Taylor Swift, to name just a few.

Besides that, Ariana would be pitted against big-time talents Macklemore & Ryan Lewis, Florida Georgia Line, Imagine Dragons, and Phillip Phillips for the New Artist of the Year Award Presented by Kohl's. Who wouldn't be nervous?

Still, Ariana was a pro. She wasn't about to let a case of nerves throw her off her game. Taking the stage in a glittering red gown, she belted out her song "Tattooed Heart" with skill and emotion, stunning the crowd before her. When she'd finished, many in the crowd gave her a standing ovation, including pop queen Lady Gaga. It was enough to give a girl an enormous ego!

Yet when Ariana won New Artist of the Year, she was far from smug. In fact, she looked shocked and overwhelmed. She leaned into her friend actress Jennette McCurdy before standing to give her a big hug. Rushing to the stage in her dress and heels, Ariana looked more like an awkward schoolgirl than a rising superstar.

Lady Gaga and R. Kelly applaud Ariana's performance at the 2013 American Music Awards.

Onstage, she humbly thanked her fans and everyone who'd helped her along the way. With only a few seconds left to speak, she pulled a list from the front of her dress, speed-reading the names on it so she wouldn't miss thanking anyone.

Breathless and gracious, she finished with even more gratitude. The win meant she had tons of support, and all her hard work was paying off. **"I love you guys so much. Thank you. This is crazy. I love you. Thank you,"** Ariana said, before hurrying off center stage.

Ariana poses with family members.

# CHAPTER ONE

# BROADWAY BABY

Ariana grew up in Boca Raton, Florida.

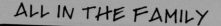

## ALL IN THE FAMILY

Ariana was born on June 26, 1993. Her full name is Ariana Grande-Butera.

Growing up in Boca Raton, Florida, Ariana loved singing, dancing, acting, and entertaining. She took up community and children's theater when she was eight and landed her first lead role in *Annie*. She also sang with symphonies and even performed "The Star-Spangled Banner" on national television. But she didn't always have a huge audience for her performances. When she experimented with stand-up comedy routines, her most frequent fans were her grandparents.

Ariana hugs her mom, Joan Grande.

When Ariana was only four years old, she called Nickelodeon studios and tried to get a role on the show *All That*.

When Ariana was eight, she got a huge boost. While on a cruise, she sang karaoke just for fun. Little did she know singer Gloria Estefan was on board listening to her belt out a song. Gloria came over afterward and encouraged Ariana to continue to pursue singing.

Gloria Estefan is a singer, songwriter, actress, and entrepreneur.

## Stage Star

Pretty soon, Ariana was trying out for roles in Broadway productions. She felt prepared for the competitive auditions. But being prepared didn't guarantee overnight success. At one audition, she was psyched to have the choreography down pat. Then, after performing the steps perfectly, she was quickly dismissed. She hadn't made some required silly faces during the dance.

Things went much better when Ariana tried out for *13: The Musical*. Thousands auditioned for only thirteen roles. And Ariana was chosen for one of them. Her victory meant she'd be working as a professional actor as a young teen. There would be no more middle school for Ariana!

Ariana and her fellow *13: The Musical* cast members rehearsed in matching T-shirts.

### STAR STUDENT

Before Ariana's career took off, she attended North Broward Preparatory School in Coconut Creek, Florida. She completed her studies through a long-distance program with the school in 2012.

Ariana had to sing and dance at the same time in 13: The Musical.

## On Broadway

Playing the part of Charlotte, Ariana didn't have a huge role in the show. As a member of the ensemble, she had only a few lines. Still, when she started rehearsals, she got a big surprise. Working on Broadway was even harder than going to school.

Every day, Ariana danced for more than twelve hours. After each rehearsal, she spent more hours trying to ease her muscle pain. Her vocal cords got a major workout too. She had to sing some super-high notes, and she had to hit them with

LINES = words spoken by an actor in a play

perfect pitch. That meant she needed to learn to breathe properly, take care of her voice, and push herself vocally. But her hard work paid off. Because of the show, her vocal range expanded.

Performing in a Broadway show may have been tricky, but Ariana was up for the challenge—no matter what it took. She spent about two years performing, mastering her new skills, and gaining confidence. When another amazing opportunity came her way, she was ready. She auditioned for a role on the Nickelodeon show *Victorious*.

## WHICH WITCH?

Ariana would love to get back to Broadway someday. A dream role of hers would be to play the wicked witch Elphaba in *Wicked*.

Idina Menzel, the original Elphaba, won a Tony Award for her performance.

# CHAPTER TWO

# VICTORIOUS, ON-SCREEN AND OFF

Ariana stands with Miranda Cosgrove of *iCarly*.

Ariana poses with Jennette McCurdy of *iCarly*.

**MEDIA =**
<u>television, radio, magazines,</u>
<u>and other methods of</u>
<u>distributing information</u>

Ariana was thrilled when producer Dan Schneider called to tell her she'd gotten the role of Cat Valentine on *Victorious*. He'd produced the shows she'd loved as a little kid, such as *All That* and *The Amanda Show*. Now, as a teenager, she'd be working with him!

Not only that, she was joining a talented cast that included Victoria Justice, Elizabeth Gillies, Avan Jogia, and Matt Bennett. The media was eager to talk to Ariana now that she was on a hit TV show. She told reporters how cast members loved to prank one another on set and hang out playing Wii or jamming together.

## SINGER-SONGWRITER

One of the first songs Ariana remembers singing is "Somewhere over the Rainbow," from *The Wizard of Oz*. And the first song she ever wrote, at the age of ten, was about rain.

When the first season of *Victorious* aired, strangers were eager to talk to Ariana too. One day, she was having lunch with her mom when a woman commented on Ariana's beautiful red hair, which Ariana had dyed for her role. Suddenly, the woman recognized Ariana as Cat. So did the woman's daughter and her daughter's friends. They screamed in excitement and then delivered a cupcake to Ariana's table.

Ariana (RIGHT) and the *Victorious* cast gather at Nickelodeon's 23rd Annual Kids' Choice Awards.

## Pursuing Her Passion

Ariana was proving to be an amazing actress and singer on *Victorious*. And she'd already shown her skills as a vocalist in a Broadway musical. But music was her lifelong passion, and she wanted to get even better. So in 2010, she started working with Eric Vetro, a vocal coach. She loved him as though he was a member of her family. And she knew she could trust him to help. He also coached Katy Perry, a singer Ariana admired for her vocal abilities and down-to-earth attitude.

Ariana and Katy Perry hung out backstage at the MTV Europe Music Awards in 2013.

17

COVER =
a performance of a song that has
been recorded by another artist

While filming *Victorious*, Ariana made several recordings of herself singing covers and released them on YouTube. They were huge hits. Since uploading her cover of Adele's "Rolling in the Deep" in August 2011, she has gotten more than 40 million views.

Those viewers must have included a few pretty important people. In 2011, Ariana had some exciting news to share. She'd signed with Universal Republic Records! And she began working on her first album.

of Performers
n.com

## GET YOUR YUM ON

With a busy schedule like hers, Ariana has to keep her energy up. Whenever she gets a chance, she munches on her two favorite foods: sushi and strawberries. In fact, she eats at least five strawberries each day!

Here are some of Ariana's top musical inspirations:
Brandy
Imogen Heap
India.Arie
Judy Garland
Whitney Houston

## Moving On—and Up

After three seasons, the cast of *Victorious* got some sad news. The show was canceled in 2012. Ariana then had a meeting with Nickelodeon producers. She hoped maybe they'd hire her to work on another show. But she never even got a chance to audition.

Ariana didn't need to audition. She'd already been chosen to star in the brand-new show *Sam & Cat*! The show was going to be a spin-off of both *Victorious* and the TV show *iCarly*. Ariana would continue her role as Cat, while actress Jennette McCurdy from *iCarly* would play Sam. Ariana was stoked!

Ariana and Jennette McCurdy present an award at Nickelodeon's Kids' Choice Awards in 2013.

CHAPTER THREE

# SUPERSTAR ON THE RISE

## DEBUT =
### first album or performance for the public

Ariana had more good news to share throughout 2013. In March, she released her debut single "The Way," which she recorded with rapper Mac Miller. It hit No. 1 on iTunes the very same day. In April, she signed with the management company Scooter Braun to push her singing career into high gear. The same company managed stars such as Justin Bieber, Cody Simpson, and Carly Rae Jepsen.

Ariana and Mac Miller performed on *Late Night with Jimmy Fallon* in 2013.

That summer, Ariana felt a little stressed as she waited for *Sam & Cat* to hit the airwaves. She knew a few people were trashing it online before they even saw it. Some people wrote that the show would be awful. But when the premiere aired, more than 4 million viewers tuned in to watch. Ariana had nothing to worry about.

## MADE-FOR-TV MOVIE STAR

Before *Sam & Cat*, Ariana starred in the Nickelodeon movie *Swindle* with Jennette McCurdy. It came out in the summer of 2013.

## Chart Topper

The release of her debut album, *Yours Truly*, in September 2013, was another success for Ariana. The album reached No. 1 on the *Billboard* 200 chart. It was the most popular album in the whole country!

### MAJOR PRAISE

Ariana finds it flattering that she's sometimes compared to singer Mariah Carey.

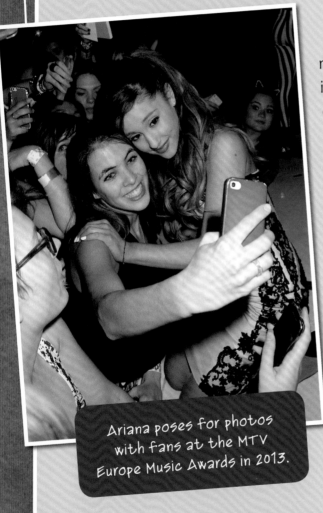

Ariana poses for photos with fans at the MTV Europe Music Awards in 2013.

Fans loved the results. But for Ariana, it represented years of hard work. In that time, her voice had matured. She had to rerecord songs that were already finished. Not that she resented any of her extra efforts. It was all part of becoming a superstar recording artist.

After releasing *Yours Truly*, Ariana had to take a break—and *not* by choice. An injured vocal cord forced her out of the recording studio and onto the couch. She rested and watched movies with a friend. In a tweet, she called it her **"first day off in forever."**

Ariana's debut album, *Yours Truly*, has sold more than 1 million copies.

Ariana and Mika perform "Popular Song" together on Dancing with the Stars.

## Loving Life

It didn't take long for Ariana to bounce back to a busy schedule though. She got started on her next album and went back to performing. In October, she performed a duet with singer Mika on the TV show *Dancing with the Stars*. And by November, Ariana was singing solo at the American Music Awards.

## GIVING BACK

Ariana offers free singing and dancing lessons to kids through her brother's charity organization, Broadway in South Africa.

Before she was awarded New Artist of the Year, Ariana opened up in an interview about life as a superstar. With two jobs—one as an actress and one as a singer—she had a jam-packed schedule and zero regrets.

"It's crazy, but it's so worth it," she said. **"I get to do everything that I love, and I'm so happy and it's really fun."**

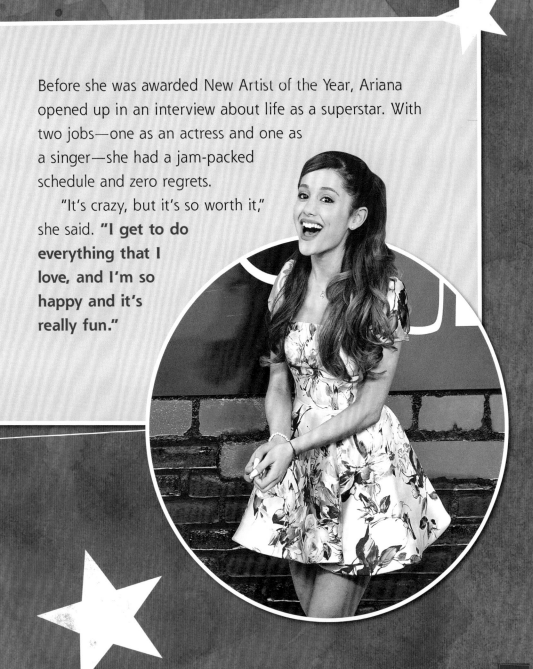

# ARIANA
## PICS!

# SOURCE NOTES

7   *American Music Awards 2013 Ariana Grand's Epic Acceptance Speech*, YouTube video, 1:27, posted by "NowWorldNews," November 25, 2013, https://www.youtube.com /watch?v=aQLY8GsXDqs.

25  Ariana Grande, *Twitter*, September 11, 2013, https://twitter.com/ArianaGrande /status/377920611605282816.

27  *Ariana Grande Red Carpet Interview—AMAs 2013*, YouTube video, 1:23, posted by "American Music Awards," November 24, 2013, https://www.youtube.com /watch?v=jSwv2gZGbC0.

# MORE ARIANA INFO

Ariana's Facebook Page
https://www.facebook.com/arianagrande
If you're a Facebook user, "Like" Ariana's page to join more than 13 million fans.

Ariana's Instagram Page
http://instagram.com/arianagrande#
Check out Ariana's stylish pics on this site.

Ariana's Twitter Page
https://twitter.com/ArianaGrande
Get up-to-the-minute updates, straight from Ariana.

Ariana's YouTube Page
https://www.youtube.com/user/ArianaGrandeVevo
Watch Ariana's videos and dance to your favorite Ariana songs.

Shaffer, Jody Jensen. *Victoria Justice: Television's It Girl*. Minneapolis: Lerner Publications, 2014.
Read this bio to learn all about Ariana's fellow cast member on *Victorious* and more details of the hit show.

Smith, Emily. *The Ariana Grande Handbook*. Queensland, Australia: Emereo, 2013.
Read this book and get the details on the superstar's life.

# INDEX

# PHOTO ACKNOWLEDGMENTS

The images in this book are used with the permission of: © Kevin Winter/Getty Images, p. 2;
© James Devaney/WireImage/Getty Images, pp. 3 (bottom), 27; © Bruce Glikas/FilmMagic/
Getty Images, pp. 3 (top), 4 (top right), 9, 20 (top), 25, 28 (right); © Jeff Kravitz//FilmMagic/
Getty Images, p. 4 (bottom), 24; © Ian Gavan/Getty Images, pp. 4 (top left), 7; © Michael Tran/
FilmMagic/Getty Images, pp. 5, 17; © Kevin Mazur/AMA2013/Getty Images, p. 6; Adam Nemser/
PhotoLink/Newscom, p. 8 (top); © FloridaStock/Shutterstock.com, p. 8 (bottom); © S. Granitz/
WireImage/Getty Images, p. 10; © Jim Spellman/Getty Images, p. 11; © Walter McBride, p. 12;
© Frank Micelotta/Getty Images, p. 13; © Angela Weiss/Getty Images, pp. 14 (bottom right),
18; © Noel Vasquez/Getty Images, p. 14 (top); © Larry Busacca/KCA2010/Getty Images, p. 16;
© Robin Marchant/Getty Images, p. 19; © Kevork Djansezian/Getty Images, p. 19; © Jamie
McCarthy/Getty Images, p. 20 (bottom left); © Timothy Hiatt/Getty Images, p. 20 (bottom right);
© Lloyd Bishop/NBC/NBCU Photo Bank/Getty Images, p. 21; © Ben A. Prunchie/Getty Images,
p. 22; © Steve Zak/FilmMagic/Getty Images, p. 23; © Lester Cohen/WireImage/Getty Images,
p. 23; © Adam Taylor/ABC/Getty Images, p. 26; © Paul Drinkwater/NBC/Getty Images, p. 28 (top
left); © David Livingston/Getty Images, p. 28 (bottom left); © Aaron Davidson/WireImage/Getty
Images, p. 29 (top middle); © Uri Schanker/FilmMagic/Getty Images, p. 29 (top right); © Jun Sato/
WireImage/Getty Images, p. 29 (top left).

Front Cover: © Steve Granitz/WireImage/Getty Images, (large image); © Troy Rizzo/WireImage/
Getty Images, (inset).

Back Cover: © David Livingston/Getty Images.


Main body text set in Shannon Std Book 12/18.
Typeface provided by Monotype Typography.